Love
COMES DOWN

Judy Belgau

God loves you & so do I! ~Judy Belgau :)

Every good gift and every perfect gift is from above.

—James 1:17 (NKJV)

ISBN 978-1-63961-680-0 (paperback)
ISBN 978-1-63961-681-7 (digital)

Christian Faith Publishing, Inc.
832 Park Avenue
Meadville, PA 16335
www.christianfaithpublishing.com

Printed in the United States of America

This book is dedicated to Jeremy and Jason, the best sons ever, and to my grandbabies, Jakobsen and Jensen, and all their cousins and siblings to come.

In the black of the night, when it's too dark to see,
God made a night-light for you and for me.
Love comes down.
God created the sun, moon, and the stars!

In the daytime, it's sunny, so we can go play.
Don't think that it's funny; God planned it that way.
Love comes down.
Thanks for all the light!

The planets, the mountains, the oceans, the plants
were made by Him, just like the hippos and ants.
Love comes down.
God made everything good. ☺

He gave to your parents all the love that they had.
Then you came as a baby to your mom and dad.
Love comes down.

"Before I formed you in the womb I knew you" (Jeremiah 1:5).

You may have uncles or aunties, sisters or brothers,
cousins, grandpas, or loving grandmothers.
Love comes down.
God made families. Yay!

He made your bright eyes that can see and your ears that can hear,
your nose that can smell and your mouth that can cheer.
Love comes down.

Hallelujah! Praise God with everything!

Your brain can remember and learn great new things.
Your body can heal all your owies and stings.
Love comes down.

The fear of the Lord
is the beginning
of knowledge.
—Proverbs 1:7

You keep growing and growing. You'll be big someday too.
That's one of God's promises He's made for you.
Love comes down.

"He who has promised is faithful" (Hebrews 10:23).

One day you'll know that God gave you *free will*.
We get the *choice* to be friends with Him still.
Love comes down.
Choose well!

The apple doesn't fall far from the tree!

Adam used his free will and sinned in the garden.
Now we do the same, and we need God's pardon.
Love comes down.

It's a serious problem the Bible does tell.
The devil is trying to lead us to hell.
Love comes down.

Don't let the devil win!

God loves us too much to put us down there.
That's why He sent Jesus to show us His care.
Love comes down.

"Believe on the Lord Jesus Christ and you will be saved" (Acts 16:31).

Can you see it? Do you know?
There's more to *this* life like where you will go.
Love comes down.

Another choice! Make it right.
Hell was not made for you!

Jesus came down from heaven for us to believe.
He died for our sins and our souls to retrieve.
Love comes down.

"He is not willing that any should perish, but that all would repent" (2 Peter 3:9).

You mean God's Son loves me and died in my place
so I can have freedom, my sins could be erased?
Love comes down.

| Before Jesus | After Jesus |

"None of the sins which he has committed shall be remembered against him" (Ezekiel 33:16).

Ask God to forgive you, and He'll always stay close by you *forever*; He *wants it that way!* Love comes down.

Dear God, please forgive me.

Believe God's true story; it's a rock-solid case.
Then when we die, He'll save us a place.
Love comes down.

"I go to prepare a place for you" (John 14:2).

Now look forward to heaven where one day you'll see
God right up close and the whole family.
Love comes down.

*"And the street of the city was pure gold, like
transparent glass" (Revelation 21:21).*

Until then, let's hide His Word in our hearts.
Pray to Him, talk with Him, as your day starts.
Love comes down.

"For God so loved the world that he gave his only begotten Son, *that whoever believes in Him* shall not perish *but have everlasting life"* *(John 3:16).* (Memorize it!)

Thanks, God, for the love!

Place your favorite photo *here.*

I love You too!

About the Author

Judy Belgau is the mother of two kids. She has been teaching Sunday school (kids ministry) for twenty-three years. She also taught sixth grade art. Her love of God and His Word, combined with her love for kids of all ages, inspired this book. Judy has a degree in fine arts. Her desire is that the Word of God and His plan of salvation will be spread through the simple reading of this book.